HEALING ON VIBRATIONAL FREQUENCIES

Ride the Wave of the Divine, Reuniting Faith and Medicine

SIEGLINDE COE MARTENS, PHD

Edited by Kristen Corrects, Inc.

Cover art design by Natasha Brown

Formatting by Giacomo Giammatteo

Picture by Tony Taffe

First edition published 2019

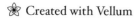 Created with Vellum

ACKNOWLEDGMENTS

Many marvelous souls have walked beside me and impacted my life. You have each been a gift in my search for my SELF.

To George, thank you for being my partner in the strong connection we have with the Divine Source. Mother Meera, I am humbled and honored to receive your guidance. Thank you to my parents, who taught me to be strong, hardworking, honest, kind, and to know that I can create anything. It is up to me and the intention I hold.

Chapter One

AN INTRODUCTION

The eternal question of *Who am I, what is my purpose?* has haunted humankind since the beginning. Because we live in a linear-thinking world with a time clock, the past is gone, the future is unknown and we scurry about trying to figure out what is going in the present. In actuality we are multidimensional beings and time is but an illusion—the past, present, and future occur simultaneously. We are able to cross over and draw from all experiences in order that our present experiences are clear and growth-producing. We are all-knowing and when we come from the womb into this low-vibrating dimension that is Earth, we fall asleep. As the soft spot in the baby's head closes, the ego is formed and we begin forgetting that we are Divine.

Through our many lifetimes, thousands upon thousands of

them, we accumulate experiences that are nothing more than charged Energy particles that are forever stored in our cellular structure. As we move through our life, we magically draw the opposing energetic charge from our memory bank as a mirror of opportunity so that we may neutralize it and move it out of our cellular structure. Nietzsche once said, "You must have chaos within to give birth to a dancing star." The dancing star filled with enchantment comes when we pay attention to the magical and the miraculous. We each must live this mystery—we cannot solve it—remembering that we are the thinker of the thought, the soul, the seer, the dreamer, the creator. It is our brain that creates the material world, the grand illusion, and the brain is the transducer of energetic vibration which moves into the experience of our senses.

A thought is all we are and it is either an interpretation or a choice. A thought is an invisible vibrational Energy which draws to it what it thinks about, thus the expression, "Only thinking makes it so." Quantum physics argues that a thought is energy filled with information. If you place a thought with intention into the electromagnetic field of the third dimension, it can do nothing but interpret itself and loop back to you. This is Universal law. When we have a thought, we have the potential of creating the internal possibility. The silent space between our thoughts are the windows to the soul, and in this silence we find God.

· · ·

Throughout time we have crippled our spirit and have lost the memory of our Divinity. This is part of the evolution of the human and our planet Earth. Humankind is still asking the universal questions:

- *Who am I?*
- *What am I?*
- *Why am I?*
- *What is my purpose?*
- *Where can I find happiness?*
- *Why do I feel lost and alone?*
- *What is my relationship with the Universe and God?*

The Indian saint Sai Baba says that if only the agony and tool of man to accumulate wealth and power are directed toward God, man can be infinitely happy. The illusion of life hides from him the face of God, which shines from every being and thing around him. Illusion is the nature of darkness and ignorance. In deep sleep, dreamless sleep, the self alone exists. You are not aware that you are God.

Our eyes are blinded by a thick veil of mist that hides the Light and the higher vibrations of the Universe and the Divine Source. Most humans today still think they are a living body when in fact they are but an electrically motivated machine that simulates life through vibrations of their soul which alone lives in the body and wills it to function. The electrically vibrating nerve wires operate bodily mechanisms entirely through automatic reflexes and instinctive control over (and to only a very minute extent) through mental decisions. The cells and organs have an electrical awareness as well and fulfill their purpose with no mental action. The heartbeat is purely automatic. White blood corpuscles in the blood move to repair injury as automatically as Pavlov's dogs salivate at the sound of a bell.

The human and its electric recording brain thinks that he thinks and lives, loves and dies. He thinks he is conscious while awake and unconscious while asleep. He does not know that consciousness never sleeps, never changes, for consciousness in man is his immortality.

Jesus said that man shall not see death, for there is no death to see or to know. Likewise the body does not live, and having never lived it cannot die. The soul alone lives. The soul is a constantly moving vibration, a wave form that cannot be destroyed. Bodily birth leads to death, to birth, to death, to birth. It is a vibrational loop. The secret to the Universe and to man's ability to merge with his soul or light body is in the raising of his vibration.

. . .

Over the last several years the vibration of the earth has shifted: The dark forces are getting darker in its chaos, negativity, violence, murder, wars, politics, and crime in general. The light is getting lighter, for those who have come as Light workers must now open and clear old patterns and pictures from their cellular memory so that they can hold the highest vibration possible.

This Shift in vibration is opening an opportunity for us to create a higher vibration so the Divine source can move in with a wake-up call (that is, if we have the ears to hear). We feel an urgency but do not always understand what this is; we act it out in different ways.

All humans are making a choice to transmute and shift to take the soul's path, or they are leaving the planet, creating illness and death or having Mother Nature in its fury create death. This can come in many ways: car accidents, air crashes, and sudden death without any explanation. It is simply the soul choosing this spiritual path.

The purpose for all humans at this time is to move Energy through the third dimension, through consciousness and out. As this is done, cells are filled with new vibrations and all humans will come together as one, as it was in the past. The Divine memory will come forth and the human will merge with their light body and the portals in this third-dimensional universe will complete and move on. Many avatars live among us now to help us wake up and reconnect with Divinity.

Together we will explore the nature of Energy and the vibration of all things. We will see how we can work with ourselves to make room for these higher vibrations. It is critical to stay away from the constant bombardment of doom and gloom, and especially toxic people in our lives. This is our birthright and the fact that we are here at this gloriously delicious time in the history of the Universe is the greatest miracle of all.

This writing will help you understand how to increase your frequency as you ascend to your personal relationship with the God who lives inside your heart.

Chapter Two

THE SEPARATION OF FAITH AND MEDICINE

Notes from *Spirituality and Healing in Medicine*, a Harvard Medical School Course

In the seventeenth century, there was a separation of mind and body. The church took the mind, science, and body. The mind became unworthy in the science arena. (It is not until our time that science returned very slowly and with trepidation to the possible mind-body connection.)

Overall health today is divided into three areas: pharmaceutical, surgery, and self-care. But what about stress, anger, high blood pressure, depression, anxiety, pain, and hormone imbalances (they lower the pain threshold and cause a lower sperm count in men and PMS, severe hot flashes, and erratic ovulation in women[1])? It is often years before these untreated symptoms manifest in breast cancers or prostate cancer. Just being told that a condition exists changes who we are and the thoughts and behavior we exhibit.

Meditation is just one step of healing. It involves two distinct steps.

1. The repetition of a word, sound, mantra, or prayer, or repetitive muscular activity.
2. Allowing the mind to let go of intruding thought.

All ancient cultures had these two steps present, always with the return to the repetition when other thoughts intrude. Christianity in the first and second century found hermits repeating the word "Jesus" on each and every out breath. In the twelfth century, monks explained this unity by focusing on the out breath. In the fourteenth century in the area of Mt. Athos, people knelt twice a day and on the out breath spoke the words "Lord Jesus," and as with the others disregarding and intrusions of thought. Fourteenth-century Spain held the focus on breathing. Islam was the same: The Dhikr-Wird, "Allah," was repeated over and over. In Taoism it was common to kneel and count each out breath up to the tenth one and then begin with one, always disregarding any thoughts that are intrusive to the ritual. Shamanistic ritual for meditation is the beating of drums and chanting. Tennison with his huge ego repeated his own name over and over. All forms of meditation were effective, creating a connection with the Divine, thereby relieving stress and creating balance.

Spirituality is feeling the presence of an energy—and it works. The people who feel Energy near and within them have fewer medical symptoms.[2] Therapy must go hand in hand with each person's individual belief system. Medicine cannot move ahead without a scientific base—this is revolutionary.

Other research at the beginning of the twenty-first century shows that nine out of ten people believe in the afterlife; six in ten believe in the devil; three in ten believe in reincarnation; two in ten believe in astrology.[3] Many Americans today are dissatisfied and their inner needs are not met. As a nation, we may be in recovery from addictions and all our isms.

We share a reaching up and out, a hunger for God. Many small groups are springing up to unite people who share a common bond. We must understand all faiths—looking at commonality, not differences—to understand that we are all one. Americans don't know what they clearly believe in creating a population vulnerable to negative religious movements.

. . .

Throughout time, opinions have been diverse. Carl Marx believed religion is the opium of the people. Freud believed religion is a universal obsession and neurosis. Jung believed that no one could be fully healed without God.

In the late 1980s, as reported in the *Byrd Southern Medical Journal*, fifty percent of patients in a coronary care unit received healing prayers from a distance; the patients did not know which group they were in. The group receiving prayer had remarkably improved overall emotional and physical health while the other group became worse.[4] In Alameda County, the Strawbridge Study, with a twenty-eight-year follow up of 5,000 people, showed great benefit across the board to all with faith.[5] Mormon men in California have half the reported cases of cancer compared to non-Mormon men, and coronary problems are dramatically less in Orthodox Jews than other men.[6]

Today, however, there is still a wall between medicine and religion. The question is: Should this wall come down? The problem is that scientific studies are confined to traditional religions. Studies do not recognize faiths that allow freedom for the individual to be responsible and to be one with God.

Let's take a look at other belief systems and how they are connected to healing.

AFRICAN HEALING

The belief system of Africa is directly linked with the deities of the skies, the sacred and ultimate power. The common customs of the continent are that disease is caused by imbalance of faith, family, ancestry, ghosts of the dead, and acts of God. Treatments are often ritualistic; the most common ritual ensures the favor of the divine and wards off evil. Rites of passage in life, birth, maturity, marriage, and death—the return to ancestors—are a powerful custom of faith, and hold together families and communities.

In African medicine, the patient is balanced with the Energy of the earth. This is a connection we have lost due to the interferences of our electronically advanced society, which interferes with our energetic systems. The patient is cured with touch therapy, music, dance, incantations, bells, or drumming. Dance is an expression of an intensified sense of life, the magical mastery over nature. The mind and body are united for healing. Patients rest in gratitude and knowledge that the Divine will provide.

In African belief systems, there are four types of healers. The diviners diagnose illnesses and imbalance, herbalists heal with roots and plants, the shrine priest performs rituals, and the Divine herbalist heals by addressing spiritual and physical conditions. Herbalists believe that like attracts like and they seek to maintain homeostasis of the body.

Payment to the healer is on a sliding scale and the medicine man asks for gifts to hold his interest. When the cure is complete, a large fee is requested but not required. What a refreshing payment plan! The emphasis is on restoring purity and removing pollution of the body, mind, and soul—not payment for services rendered—so the person can return to a normal life.

Africa is a continent with a sense of community. Be your brother and your sister healer. The simplicity and beauty of life and tradition is what our heart longs for so desperately.

TIBETAN AND BUDDHIST HEALING

Buddhism has never opposed science; the essence of this belief system is to cultivate the truth in an unsaturated mind. When healing, the focus is on exposing the imbalance by decreasing the pain in the empty spaces of the atom or the gap. The patient begins to gain the ability to expand the gap. This reduces their anxiety and the therapist helps the patient dissolve the pain into the mind's empty space. Now new Energy is formed to fill the space.

. . .

To create the unsaturated mind—whose purpose is to blend with the nature of consciousness, becoming one with what the mind is focused on—one must have tremendous motivation. The therapist must be at one with what the patient is revealing. Rid the mind of memory and desire, leaving only faith and expectation. To do this, concentrate on one single object; this acts as an anchor.

An unsaturated mind is expectant and curious without preconceived ideas. It is the faith and curiosity that not allows the mind to be a magnet drawing the fragmented material to the patient into cause and effect. Moving from saturated to unsaturated requires that the preconceptions are not fully conceived by the therapist until there is a full birth and blending between the two people. It must be spontaneous, not mechanical.

Meditation creates the mystical mind when one experiences his or her breath. One must be in a relaxed state, where he or she is in touch with the self. Awareness is the receptivity of thought and images. It's necessary to concentrate and not get distracted.

The Buddhist definition of faith its trust and confidence beyond the known, and the experience of Oneness with the Divine.

JEWISH HEALING METHODS

Judaism believes that healing takes place in the context of community alongside the best traditional medicine. The sacred is brought from the community into the home. There is an ever-evolving theology whereby the individual can find his own journey toward health.

The primary tool for healing again is the community. It is an obligation. Ritualistic prayers are seen as power in words and in song. This is also true of people with a broken spirit. Judaism is rich with resources and support, with many chants that free the mind and energize the spirit. One hundred blessings a day must be said for a variety of applications. Prayers are sent to the master of the Universe for all things. Psalms are the most personal of all text. The Energy of these psalms have been in the Universe for thousands of years.

CATHOLIC SPIRITUAL PRACTICES

Healing is an ongoing process of touching, soothing, and elevating the disease in the body, mind, and spirit. In Catholicism, health is defined as the absence of a diagnosis or the presence of a fullness of life, the ability to function in its highest form. Spirituality gives ultimate meaning and purpose in life; therefore, spiritual care must be included in the menu of services provided so that all may be well in America.

· · ·

Jesus' ministry is one of healing the ill and relationships. For Catholics, ritual is a very important aspect of everyday life with elements of familiarity, repetitiveness, and spirituality. The person when anointed has a connection with the community of the church, especially with the laying on of hands, forehead, the sign of the cross.

Confession is another opportunity of healing. In the old days it was referred to as penance and guilt, although now it is the sacrament of conciliation—the healing of relationships—under the seal of confession and confidentiality. Devotional rituals, the rosary, and the Hail Mary are sources of healing; the prayers are directed to individual saints for their specific healing. In my opinion, the centering prayer in group is very healing and leads to results of experiencing life in its richest form. It is wonderful to hear the paradigm shift in the church, in particular the lessening of control over the individual.

ISLAMIC SPIRITUAL HEALING PRACTICES

Spirituality is not owned by religion—it is a reversal driving force behind everything. How great this Energy is as it moves stars and galaxies! This Energy is the void of God; it is beyond limitation.

All people are on an individual journey back to God. Islam teaches how to heal; the prophetic medicine teaches how to heal by using the force, the Energy of the Divine. The human body receives and reflects Energy. You can feel emotions and feelings; you can deflect it and give your Energy to others. We are polluting ourselves through the negativity in our minds and hearts.

Islam uses subtle breath in the body generated by the organs. With this subtlety, Islam teaches the heightened sense of perception: to see angels without eyes, to smell without a nose. Our bodies can send out electrical impulses that bring us into balance.

Subtle layers exist within the body. The forehead is the focal point; science uses labor and Islam uses rituals to heal through the focus of Light in the third eye. Science and spirituality go together; each has its function.

God has created a medicine for all disease. If you have a sickness, the prophets say to use medicine and ritualistic prayer and Energy. The Divine must support you if you ask for it—this is the law of the Universe and an Islamic ritual.

Energy—and the process of harnessing it—changes the metabolic system in the body, thereby changing the body's chemistry and healing its ills. It is like a waterfall that gives Light and Energy. If you channel this in the heart, the Energy behind all things, this angelic power, then you will be whole.

According to Islamic belief, everything comes together to create a universal language for all Energy because this is all there is. It is like an atomic reaction. When one atom is split, there is a tremendous Energy. Using Energy to heal works faster because of its inherent power. People must remain open to study all and learn more about everything, and in this way, peace may be closer at hand.

HISPANIC PENTECOSTAL HEALING PRACTICES

Pentecostal revival occurred in Los Angeles and is now a community expanding throughout the world. The model for its healing is rooted in the Old Testament—a God who binds our brokenness and roundedness. He is the model for a ministry of grace. There are good and bad angels and spirits and God moves in and out through them as he chooses. There is no direct relationship with the Divine force but the force forges the relationship with the Holy Spirit, the person who comes through the Holy Spirit, Jesus.

When medicine is not available, God is depended upon and prayed to. We have access by grace, not because we are spiritual. Testimony is important because God hears. Understanding of healing is multidimensional—we are complex and not only physical; God responds to all parts of this multidimensionality. God can cure disease. Healing must, however, include spiritual well-being so it is an ongoing process. Healing attends to our brokenness.

It is fascinating to me to hear this message assuming we are imperfect and broken. How can we be one and a part of God and not be whole in our imperfections?

HEALING PRACTICES WITH EMPHASIS ON FLORENCE NIGHTINGALE

Between 1820 and 1910, Florence Nightingale practiced natural healing methods. She created the blueprint for sanitary reform. When you create sanitary conditions, health is enhanced; therefore, creating sanitary conditions is a spiritual act.

Nightingale's approaches were influenced by the mystics from all over the world. She seemed to be deeply influenced by Hindu religion. The core of the human inner nature is the Divine spark of God; until this is awakened we are not fully alive and whole.

Meditation evoking relaxation allows us to access the Divine source. Hospitals are raging with fear, prohibiting a Divine experience. Anything that achieves peace within the patient is vital. Inner guide imaging accesses a wisdom that lies beyond our personal wisdom and is very appropriate for cancer patients. If we practice this ourselves we can teach it with integrity and with more power, as it becomes a form of spiritual care. The care of the physical body is critical because it is the vehicle of the soul. Breathing exercises are sacred. Nightingale felt that since the Universe is lawful, we will feel the effects of these wrong choices (i.e., not participating in meditation).

Nightingale believed in intervention of physical pain. Pain is associated with constricted time; thus, learning to change our experience of time from linear to non-time through spirituality will support pain management. She called our essence the God consciousness within us, this inner urge to wholeness that will lead us back to God. The physical does not have to be the valley of tears if we only make the effort. Healing touch—move the chi—and you are simply the facilitator clearing the obstruction of Energy. Energy moves through us. We are the workers. We are the conduit, not the source.

EFFECTS OF INTERCESSORY PRAYER

In my experience, most people who pray are not white and do not speak English. Prayers are sent to the Universe; they do not come within an institutionalized house of worship. Prayer is to the absolute, the All, God, or whatever you want to call it. Prayers are for petition, for intercession, for adoration or confession.

We think the brain is a local organ, so it seems that thinking cannot go beyond its own hemisphere. What is the brain but a computer made of meat? We are up against a lot if we think that our thoughts impact mass consciousness. Yet this is how mass consciousness is formed in the first place. We are experiencing through the intellectual indigestion at the thought of sending Energy from a distance.

THE PSYCHOLOGY AND PHYSIOLOGY OF PAIN AS IT RELATES TO SPIRITUAL PRACTICES

Pain teaches us that we are not listening to our self—and self is the key to our soul. Chronic pain by definition is a medical failure; in my opinion, prescription drugs are directly linked to all chronic pain, and in an indirect way, individuals subconsciously want the pain because it rewards them on some level. Sensory perception of pain can be reduced as one becomes accustomed to the pain.

Acute pain has predictable characteristics. Generally speaking, acute pain generates anxiety, and triggers an emotional response first, then it is triggered in the brain. Functional disruptions go on forever, then come the depression and stress. The actual pain receptors are altered, sometimes permanently, and biological changes occur in the patient. These changes don't show up on MRIs and related tests. Now, in addition, the doctor can't find what's wrong. What is the underlying cause of the pain?

Attempts at pain management today focus on pathophysiological aspects and ignore the actual physical sensations of pain. It is the difference between noise and annoyance. We are surrounded by a lot of noise. Pain is much like the annoyance one feels. Pain is always the product of physical and emotional reactions (included here is anxiety, depression, stress, and negativity), and pain is now augmented as these emotions build. Attention must be paid to the psychology of the suffering.

Pain in necessary and suffering is *optional*. Man is not diminished by suffering, but by suffering without meaning.

Cultural background and belief systems temper reactivity to pain. Abandoning belief systems within a framework of spirituality seems to be the key to overcoming chronic pain. There is an underlying biology—the more beta power in the brain (created by the relaxation response without them knowing it) teaches chronic pain sufferers to lower their breathing while focusing on a sound, a word, or a phrase. This beta increase decreases the pain.

. . .

Investigating faith and biology, the integration of medicine and spirituality is the way of the future. When science studies the role of belief in medicine it used to be related to psychology alone. Now it is moving in the direction of the spiritual aspects and is not as easily researched but much more apparent when used.

In a similar vein, cognitive therapy suggests that as things occur in the world, we filter them and our reaction is dependent on the filters we use. People must be shown the distortions in the filter. We personalize it and say negative things to ourselves, unaware of the profound effects this has on us. They are counterproductive. Psychological therapies must be incorporated with biological medicine.

How does this relate to spirituality? Two men had serious back pain, both had surgery, both had serious pain, both were in a psychological support group. One man believed he could never be the man he once was. After two months of work his mood changed and his belief system changed because he still had will. He became a good housefather and cook. He found the will and joy to go on.

The other man was not making progress, frowned and was

cynical of the psychology of the work. One day he had a smile on his face. He told the group what happened to him. His wife was religious and he was not. A Bible fell on the floor and it opened to a page that read, *God will never test you beyond a point you can bear.* The challenge is to incorporate a person's belief systems and filters into the existing model of medicine.

THE PLACEBO EFFECT ON HEALING AND THE POWER OF BELIEF

The placebo effect is powerful and has a direct effect on healing. This could well be the answer to turning thought into healing. Placebo is a Latin word meaning *I shall please.*

One can say that the history of medicine is the history of the placebo effect: During the rituals of leeching and picking, purging, and taking parts of the criminal brain, within all this people were getting better only because they believed they would.

Placebo works because of belief of the patient, the facilitator, and the relationship of the two people's unified belief. Until the 1850s there were no drugs, only cures found in nature. Then vitamins became curable tools. In Toronto in the early 1920s, insulin treated diabetics and kept people alive. In 1929 England penicillin cured pneumonia, again without a belief. Surgery kept pace with this.

. . .

Today, life can be extended through miraculous medicine. All forms of medicine were largely dependent on the placebo effect. In 1911 doctors only came from scientifically based schools; this is when the separation occurred. Mind-body healing were no longer and the placebo was replaced with drugs.

The belief system can create the pain and the cure. Beliefs lead to life and to death yet are left out of medicine. Much of modern medicine is a part of the placebo effect.

What does God have to do with all this? We think we are the smartest and most powerful people. We have learned that we will die and this fear creates negative emotions. Not one culture up until today has not believed in the afterlife. There is something beyond and we are genetically wired to such belief. We are wired for God.

Why is it that we're all here believing in the power of belief, yet we are so biased as we view changes through our filter of belief?

SPIRITUALITY AT THE BEDSIDE

Imagine this: There is a great feast in both Heaven and Hell, and in Heaven the people are feeding one another. This is an analogy of where we are in evolution. It is time to reach out and touch. This must begin with each one of us. Even when held rigid, the higher power provides solace especially at the bedside.

The word *heal* means to restore a rift between us, restore balance, to bind back. Medicine and religion are linked if we are to be true healers. Energy is the life breath derived from a power that overlooks all things; we personalize this Energy through our beliefs and practices. All meanings are derived from the human attachments to the Divine. The brain is sculpted through our experience and belief. We self-create our limitations.

Spirituality and science must be synthesized: faith seeking understanding and understanding seeking faith. Patients need a sense that is purpose and meaning. Only faith will create this purpose. Faith comes from our feeling of separation from our parent, God. Fears of death are always expressed in human terms: "I won't watch my children grow up." In truth is this not an inexpressible need to know we are finally going back to our real home, leaving the illusion behind until we come back to do it all over?

The connection between the brain and heart has to be felt in the attachment area, the heart. To me, this separation of mind and heart is an overlay of the division between science and faith. It is interestingly confusing since what we think is real in our Universe is but the illusion.

Let us delve into the unseen and create this paradigm shift. It is our individual birthright to feel the Divine and walk steadfastly through our dimensional experience.

---

1. Kang, Hey-Joo, Pak Chung, and Raymond Chang. "Alternative Medicine and Female Infertility." *Reproductive Endocrinology and Infertility* (2007): 189.

2. Gerber, Richard, MD, *Vibrational Medicine*, 1988. Santa Fe, NM: Bear & Company.

3. Shermer, Michael, *How we believe: The search for God in an age of science,* 2000. Macmillan.

4. Contreras, Francisco, *The Hope of Living Cancer Free,* 1999. Sioloam Press.

5. Koenig, Harold G., Ellen Idler, Stanislav Kasl, Judith C. Hays, Linda K. George, Marc Musick, David B. Larson, Terence R. Collins, and Herbert Benson. "Religion, spirituality, and medicine: a rebuttal to skeptics." (1999): 123-131.

6. Jarvis, George K., and Herbert C. Northcott. "Religion and differences in morbidity and mortality." *Social science & medicine* 25, no. 7 (1987): 813-824.

Chapter Three

VIBRATIONAL FREQUENCIES

Twelve Frequencies in the Universe

The Divine Source created itself as the vibrational essence of itself. All is Energy and vibration and created twelve frequencies. These original twelve frequencies of Light are in all things and in the Universe. These twelve could differentiate each other so that the experience of the One (God) was complete and could know itself.

Our third dimension is the slowest vibration in our unlimited Universe, and it is who you are and what you can be. There is nothing outside that we need to experience to find out who we are. There is only the One, and this is the place to search for answers. The One has sent a signal that it is time to harvest all that has been planted. The physical shift is speeding up in all dimensions.

What does this tell us about the state of being human? Is it any wonder that greed, lies, lust, inhumanity to one another, sex sales of children, killing, wars, the thirst for money, power, and worse are the nature and a part of the world we attempt to thrive in? Humanity believes they are supreme beings, yet we don't even use more than ten percent of our brain.

We must use our Energy with *intention*. There is tremendous work to do. The physical and the electromagnetic field cannot shift without being clear. The old pictures of who our ego made us out to be must be released on a cellular level and replaced with a higher vibration, the vibration of the One. All humans will experience themselves as a single group and the portal of the Universe will open and once again return to the One. Death is an exciting time and a habit we recall in its Divine perception.

Birth, on the other hand, is very difficult—we forget who we truly are and have to be filled with something. This is when our hard drive is filled with our earthly belief systems, assumptions, decisions, actions, and results. This comes from our family and world around us filling us with the belief systems of the time. We become our program and make choices for our life, resulting in many dead ends, and too often feel like a victim of circumstance.

LIGHT LANGUAGE

The One is Light, and all comes from One. The language of Light is filled with information and the yet-untapped secrets of our Universe. This Light is hidden in our cellular structure and contains all.

Did you know every organ and every single piece that holds our meaty inside together holds an emotion? If we knew the ABCs of that, we could easily heal ourselves by understanding the emotion we are blocking, abusing, living too much or too little. Fear, for example, is held in the kidneys, anger and rage in the liver and the gallbladder. The intestine is where our grief lies.

Instead we are brainwashed to feel less than whole by being taught to learn, learn, learn, and learn some more, never to question what we are learning. When will schools ever teach us to *remember*—because all wisdom is already inside of us. Might this be why we can only access ten percent of our brain?

Some remembering takes place as we clear and raise the vibrational essence: The Light comes in through the first and second dimension and into our cells in subatomic particles. This is the Energy or vibration of the One, the Divine, God, Buddha, the Light, or the source. When the old information is released, the Divine information has room to come forth.

Our physical structure brings in physical information from the One's essence. The electron path around the atom carries all information in the third dimension. Here the releasing work must be done. Many people are resonating to the fourth and fifth dimensions already—they are classified as nutters by many. As photons move through this Universe, through all things and through the human body and hits an atom, this atom must have been cleared by us, so that when hit by the photon, the information from the Source can be downloaded with a higher vibration, from which information will come to us.

Understanding computers and how to edit, download, input, and delete, this should be familiar stuff for us. We just don't get the connection between it and us. This downloading cannot occur if we have not released on a cellular level.

CHANGES IN OUR ELECTROMAGNETIC STRUCTURE

At present we each have seven chakra systems. Each one vibrates to and is stimulated by sound and color. Each center holds a different vibration: that of Light, intuition, communication, love, emotion, creativity/reproduction, and survival. Each chakra spins like a vortex with the tip in the body shooting out the front and the back. Like a spinning flute it gets bigger as it shoots out, always round in nature. It is always seeking its point of balance or rest in the center, which is within the body itself—the zero point. These Energy centers each have their own color: red, orange, yellow, green, blue, purple, and white. Chakras can get blocked and some shoot out farther and some are more stubby in nature depending on what is going on in the body. If you are having stomach cramps the yellow chakra will use some of its Energy to heal the issue. If one has eyes to see this, it is an easy way to diagnose physical and emotional issues in that moment.

As our process of clearing speeds up and our vibrational spin increases, there is also the beginning of a change in our chakra system. We are moving into a two chakra system the Alpha and the Omega. In time, the bottom three chakras will merge together forming the Omega; the higher three chakras from the heart to the self will become the Alpha. In the shifting of the One, the higher vibrations will be better acclimated in the physical body and the human will also have, once again—as in the beginning—twelve or more connected strands of DNA. (It is actually a merging of the twelve original vibrations which broke off from the One in the very beginning. It is a merging with the One.) There are exciting times ahead; let us hope there is still time left on the clock.

. . .

This is when humans experience an understanding of who they are and know themselves as each other. This process is happening now in the cellular structure of many (known as conscious manifestors) and will surface in a short time. Awakening to an understanding of higher vibrational frequencies is an exciting time in one's life; during times like this it may be grand to venture into another life once again—this time without the forgetting of who am I, why am I here, what am I supposed to do, remembering all. This I may choose. Until then, the world where our soul lives after death sounds great to me. (By the way, did you know your soul holds all memories of all lives you have experienced and will tag along if you choose another ride in the flesh?)

Mantras and meditation will release old pictures and emotions on a subconscious level. Let's focus on keeping our heads out of it. If the old stored memory went into the cells as trauma, fear, or pain, it must be released with a similar emotion (and sometimes with health issues). It is also possible that we bring in Energy from other dimensions during the clearing process. In the releasing process, if we find ourselves crying our eyes out then we know it is working. Unexplained health issues may also happen. Look at the emotion held in the part of the body that is out of balance and you can then focus on that emotion and remember what happened in your past lives. Embrace this and make up a new story that works for your highest good. Being exceptionally tired can also be a sign. The body is actually rearranging crystalline structures to make room for more Light. All sixty-four vibrational levels can be tapped into, bringing forth information into the dimension we have grown into.

OUR THREE BODIES

Our first body is our physical body and our nonphysical electromagnetic body, which vibrates out from the physical. In the body you experience your *self* as solid and a moving object. The non-physical is equally present and can be felt and photographed. We can frame and display this person we think we are.

Our second body is made of unconditional love in our dimension. It is what was used to get here from the One. It is not about values or judgements associated with lower vibrations. Unconditional love is within the core structure of our soul. It is the conduit through which we came here. We all have the experience of this within our cellular memory.

The third body is the God or One body. It is the actual vibration of God and in the bringing together of these three bodies. One can begin the path of creation and manifestation. It is only our assumption that we cannot create, and it is this assumption that prevents us from creating. As our vibration increases, the soul comes forth and with intention we can merge. By measuring the quality of what we do, one experiences the being that you are. This determines where you are on your path and measures growth and enlightenment. All work is done alone within.

Let's look for a moment how it is that we have such thick layers of old Energy. As Energy moves from the One into the dimension—be it three, four, five, or more—it moves through our electromagnetic field and body. We have a physical experience of the vibration and thinking takes place after that. Now we react, judge, evaluate... If we do not allow the vibration to move through, we create an emotion. Emotion is the trapping of vibration in the physical and non-physical body.

In the trapping through judgement, a block or holding has been created, which gives rise to pictures or unrelated Energy patterns. How many millions of times have we judged and held these emotional charges? It is no wonder happiness and balance elude many.

The focus is sadly on a brainwashing agenda, feeding fear because it sells and controls, teaching made-up "facts." People are seduced by Facebook and the many other addictions available. Each person can be molded to fit the perfect follower by those in power. Then comes an outcry to create the solution for the problem created in the first place. I hope there is time for a massive eye-opener soon so we don't become a homogenized, sexually and emotionally robotic species that will buy into anything that provides instant gratification.

The more people who wake up, the faster the speed-up of implementing higher vibrational frequencies. I think you see where we are headed unless we begin to understand vibrations, frequency, and how to use them.

Wake up...you are a God: Generator, Operator, Destroyer.

ATLANTIS TO THE PRESENT

In Atlantis the ego got out of control and we moved into a technical war, which destroyed our land mass. An entire civilization died. This energetic vibration moved into the meteorite belt and stayed in dimensions as group consciousness. Next time the same group decided to try it again but this time we destroyed all plant life and starved to death as a group. We then went into spirit and thought it over. Our egos got out of control before the consciousness was raised and evolved.

Sound familiar? Because of this discovery, it was decided that the next time people would be kept apart by oceans, mountains, colors, and races. This was the creation of the Tower of Babble.

In our time the ego is controlled by more—again, a big part of the end game. They control and can take it. A few on our planet who have it all are bored and are now playing with mind control, genetic experimentation, germ warfare, and such. In our time, on this planet, we have come to witness the great split. There will be two distinct groups: the conscious and the unconscious. The conscious will all move into light body within the next three or four generations and merge once again into the One. This is the Light-accentuated group. The other group are the unconscious. Death will occur and the souls will evolve elsewhere. This is the group who will continue to live in ego. This is the negative-accentuated.

Both groups have already chosen their spiritual path; only a vibrational difference separates them. We who choose more experience will be going on to Venus, already prepared. (This planet is lovely, like pink cotton candy, very light, floaty in nature, and full of love vibrations. I have gone to a place like this in my meditations for at least fifteen years and never wanted to leave, thinking it was a star and only in my mind. Or was it? Now it is clear and I have come to learn that this is truly Venus.) Our Earth, however, has turned into a bottle-neck because the human fell in love with the physical density too much and got hooked on itself. The ego is running the show. Earth was never meant to be a cosmic kindergarten.

Again, we come back to the importance of raising our vibration. It is a choice and the only way to move into the Light of the One.

All spirits must pass through the earth's funnel. Beings from other galaxies have wanted to control Earth for this reason. We must now grow and increase our vibrational frequency and transmute, or the Universe itself cannot take its next step. All eyes are on us and we are given tremendous assistance and given a very serious kick.

THE ILLUSION OF MOTION

Our vibrational Universe of motion moves relentlessly to find rest, but never finds it. The human is in the same state. All matter in violent motion stimulates rest and balance through violent motion. The more violent the motion, the greater the illusion of rest and balance.

Motion can cease but it can never rest. Have we not all noticed the changes of Mother Earth herself? Violent Earth and weather changes occur daily to shed our negativity and pollution. We are not talking "climate change," a man-made concept to once again distract us from truth—all weather is cyclical and nature and will repeat itself over time. There is, however, much man-made manipulation of many things including weather when a disturbance is needed to influence the good opinions of another. If one digs into the shallow hole, is it not all about power, money, control, and instilling a fear in the hearts of people. Fear sells. The earth is our mirror so we might see our own internal storm of fear. It has been said that our environment is but a symptom of our personal and individual disease. War is only inside of us, a reflection of our anger and hate. It is a teacher for those brave souls willing to be her student.

All the planets revolve around their central sun, which is moving with incredible speed despite appearing to be at rest. Likewise, all stars move at terrific speeds to adjust their mutual unbalances in our dual universes of divided pressure. The book on the table, the couch on which we sit, the entire house full of seemingly motionless matter—all appear to be at rest, but are only simulating rest through violent motion of their many parts. Tremendous vibration may be in the tea kettle when empty of water. Nothing can manifest what it stimulates without the incredible speed of the atoms which forever rotate and revolve to make the illusion of rest possible.

All matter is the motion of Light. All motion is expressed in waves. All Light waves are mirrors that reflect each other's condition onto the furthermost star. Ours is an electrically conditioned wave universe forever seeking to go home to Oneness. For this reason all sensation responds to all other sensation; there is no empty space.

Is this a difficult concept to understand? The human confusion lies in his long assumption of the reality of matter. "If I can touch it or see it then it is real."

NULL ZONES CREATE THE NEW

Let's examine how this illusion of matter can be applied to the human and his shift into a higher vibration. Today I was walking into the supermarket and suddenly heard a loud noise of things shattering. I turned down the aisle and saw a group of people staring at an older lady who must have touched the shelves holding pots, candles, and other glassware. Mary, I'll call her, was kneeling on the floor embarrassed, frantically picking up the shattered pieces. Her hand was bleeding, clearly a result of the shattered glass. Beside her, her husband peeled off each bar code saying, "We have to pay for this."

What a sad scene. Someone had a mishap, and all eyes were on her. When I knelt beside her to help, a man approached us and said, "Leave it, we will pick this up. Let's get your information, so we can go to the hospital and have that wound in your hand looked at."

Mary looked at him and said, "But I have to pay for this."

"No ma'am, I'm the manager and we have insurance for this. You don't have to pay anything. Let's get you taken care of."

Close your eyes and imagine God doing the same for you—collecting the pieces of your broken heart from all the missteps and blows that life has thrown at you. God will heal your wounds and your sins and mistakes will be forgiven. This is the warranty called *grace*, that when you accept God and ride the higher frequencies, you can continue on your way.

Solara's 1996 book *How to Live Large on a Small Planet* speaks of null zones. They are apparently established after there has been an expansion or flowering outwards of Energy which receives some sort of a blow or shock, causing it to collapse inward upon itself. This would be in line with the fact that we live in a two-way universe: Light, which is inwardly directed toward gravity, charges mass and discharges space. When directed toward space, it charges space and discharges mass. All direction of force in nature is in a spiral. The old established Energy patterns have now been broken. There is no way that they will return to their previous patterning. They have been irrevocably changed.

The energetic vibration of a Null Zone feels jagged and raw. There is much hurt and pain. Null Zones can occur in a defined geographical area. Wars create them, as does political upheaval, economics, distress, famine, and disease. (Looks like there will always be null zones.) It's the shattering of a world or a belief system, a long-held desire, or sometimes an important relationship. This shattering creates the perfect foundation for the introduction of something entirely new. A change to replace the void within the vibration of the One and move up a notch.

The potential for rebirth from the ashes of a Null Zone is enormous.

Let's create a bit of reality as a foundation. To know God, the One, directly is extremely rare. Enlightenment occurs to less than one percent in more than ten million people. True teachers are few. God is present in all things and available at all times. God is beyond all opposites of good or bad, right or wrong, win or lose. Like the sun, all are shined upon equally. When in His presence, one experiences profound peace, stillness, and calm. This state is so powerful that any remaining ego is melted.

. . .

Examples of null zones can be found in former Yugoslavia, ex-
Soviet Union, ex-Eastern Germany, Rwanda, Burundi, Soma-
lia, and Algeria. Countries are in recovery, having had the
opportunity for mass consciousness are Cambodia, Lebanon,
Tibet, Afghanistan, Haiti, Northern Ireland, China, Ethiopia.
Potential future null zones include the United States, Mexico,
Egypt, Israel, France, and India.

Geographical null zones are like black holes and vibrationally
draw Energy into themselves. When the vibration is released,
the human population has the opportunity to learn and take a
giant leap. Null Zones are created by Mother Earth through
earthquakes, hurricanes, floods, volcanoes, and other so-called
acts of God. These are extremely useful opportunities to
release the old cellular memory and replace it with vibrationally higher attitudes, value systems, habits, and life
patterns. To experience a natural disaster is a grand opportunity to master the art of surrendering and breaking through
into something new. All things happen for a purpose and it is
always for your highest good.

Learn to embrace and welcome pain and change. You have
been freed from the old stagnant patterns and can leap into a
deeper sector of the unknown. You are forever safe in the

womb of the new and the time for birthing your Divine magnificence has come.

As T.H. Huxley said, "Sit down before fact as a little child, be prepared to give up every preconceived notion, follow humbly wherever and to whatever abysses nature leads, or you shall learn nothing. I have only begun to learn content and peace of mind since I have resolved at all risks to do this."

Chapter Four

VIBRATIONS AND BRAIN MAGNETS

The human body is nothing but a wave front pattern. Everything is only a vibrational rate in the form of a pattern. All objects are patterns. Where the wave fronts impinge there is an object. It is here, where I wish to share my personal experience with vibrational consciousness raising.

In 1994 I met Robert, a scientist, inventor, aero-space physicist, humanitarian, and a very dear friend. Robert works with the management of the wave front patterns, and he invented a generator that creates a vortex. My signature is placed into the vortex which sends Energy into the parallel Universe and finds my light body; the light body is coupled to me through the earth, through my electromagnetic field, and my physical body. The unique imprint is found. This is an overlay of the quantum biofeedback systems, one of which I use to balance a person's body at a distance. The information is put in the system and the soul's footprint is found and leads in the balance.

When Robert couples the light body to me through the earth, through my electromagnetic field, and to my physical body, two loops of Energy are created and my light body is connected with all others. Mass consciousness and the Universe get a little jolt and change their vibration as mine is raised a bit. Imagine the possibilities if several million humans raised their vibration just a bit today! We might no longer recognize the world as we know it.

Robert electromagnetically stimulates the brain magnets and boosts the human's vibration. These brain magnets are crystalline in nature and were discovered recently. This is a very exciting time and many more such things will emerge. We each have seven billion brain magnets, each having a nerve ending that has never been activated. Microscopic magnets have been found in the human brain that might explain possible links between cancer and electromagnetic fields, scientists said.

"They are little biological bar magnets made of crystals of the iron mineral magnetite," according to geobiologist Joseph L. Kirschvink, of the California Institute of Technology. The crystals are strongly magnetic, unlike other iron compounds in the body. They come in two sizes, about one-millionth and ten-millionths of an inch wide. Homing pigeons, whales, salmon, honey bees, and some shellfish and bacteria have microscopic magnets. EMFs are invisible electric and magnetic force fields generated by power lines, appliances, TV, and everything electrical—which is just about everything today, disturbing these tiny magnets.[1] However there is no convincing evidence that these internal magnets can sense the earth's magnetic field.

On a trip to my home Robert had invented his V-Gen, which keeps these EMF frequencies at bay, protecting us. We drove around testing how far from the center location of a V-Gen these rays were safe and away from disrupting us.

It turned out that it was always a six-mile radius from its center location. I had one in my home and kept one battery charged in my car at all times. Every little bit helps. We must at some point take responsibility and become educated in how we are manipulated and damaged by this man-made world. Given we use so little of our brain, we can at least take responsibility that our brain does not completely shrivel up and disrupt our vibrational connection to all that is.

Robert has scientifically documented, tested, and proved that these brain magnets are not only detecting the earth's seven frequencies, but are vibrating all the time.

When our brain magnets resonate with the vibration of the earth, we experience reduced psychological stress and a balance in our blood chemistry. The earth is designed to do this; unfortunately as was mentioned in the article, the man-made electromagnetic interference keeps us from tuning in. What a leap for the other side, right? The brain sensors are meant to feel the subtle frequencies of the earth's field since thirty percent of our Energy comes from these fields. Not only are we as humans running around stressed to the max but our energetic tank is always thirty percent empty in its optimal state.

EARTH'S SEVEN FREQUENCIES

The human vibration is one to seven. The Tibetan monks, when in deep meditation, vibrate at a ten but in their normal state they move back to seven. When the human moves to a frequency of ten he must stay at that level and integrate completely until the never-before-activated brain magnets open, hold the vibration, and then close the switch. The newly raised vibration is now permanent.

What does this all mean? Let's look at the earth's seven frequencies.

. . .

We all know that our planet has magnetic lines of force extending from its north pole to its south pole. But, they are not just static magnetic flux lines of force, they are dynamic— they vibrate at seven different rates! We refer to these as seven different frequencies. Our bodies also are in constant wave form and vibrate at frequencies of one to seven. We are all beautiful spinning light bodies that sparkle like the light in a prism. It is our light body in the other dimensions which create our Energy patterns, and the form and condition of our physicality. A force field reaching from our third dimension into the unseen cosmic world connects us to our light body.

These fields can be scientifically recorded, monitored, and photographed. Each one of us chooses three of the seven Earth frequencies to resonate with. By the age of twenty these three are securely established and usually don't change. They are:

1. Self-expression.
2. Self and others including the Energy of love.
3. Self, others, and the world around us.
4. Balance point and desire.
5. Seeking of Energy patterns as musicians, scientists, artists, dancers, writers.
6. Universal love, in search of this love.

7. Spirit connection between this world and the unseen world.

The first three are the physical energies and the last three are of spirit; the fourth is the balance point.

VIBRATIONAL CONSCIOUSNESS RAISING, A PERSONAL EXPERIENCE

My Earth frequencies turned out to be two, five, and seven. I was experiencing another unknown leap of faith. It was 5:00 PM and for ninety minutes I drank water and monitored what I was experiencing in this body. My hands and feet tingled, the inside of my left palm felt as if needles were stuck in it, my face and chin became hot and tingly, my tongue felt swollen. This body felt like putrefied matter swinging from a flagpole. It felt like suspended motion at the same time. While attempting to write what was going on during the session, my spelling was a mess of letters that made no sense. Nothing was coming in the normal sequence.

Moving from seven to ten in vibration is the first quantum leap. The others were not as intense during the actual session. The vibration of ten is about learning to create with thought and assume full responsibility for every thought. It is creating with others and the emotions. Stabilizing at ten is an emotional balance.

. . .

The time between increasing vibrations was always spent integrating and releasing. Many gut-wrenching times were spent looking so deeply into the shadow self, letting go of patterns that cling on, can be difficult and painful. Just when you think something is released it roars into a full-blown experience once again. Each time this happens it is more intense as if to say, *How much of this are you going to do?*

When the new vibration stabilizes, a door closes behind you and the only choice is to move forward and through the heartache of any issues. Some experiences may force you to relive changing relationships, let go of friends, while creating healthy relationships or new careers, dealing with feelings of loss, and not knowing what will happen next. This is all a part of this transformative process of change. Not knowing or caring what happens next is the greatest. As long as our intention is strong and the focus on the highest good, all is well and the mind can take a vacation and stop thinking about every little thing—and, worse than that, believing it can figure everything out. (The Buddha would have quite a huge belly laugh here!)

I became conscious of my dreams and asked every night to be shown the answers; this I began to trust without having to understand it. My meditations became more powerful and I slowly felt safe in my skin. The more we choose change, the more the Universe showers us with our own thoughts. Fifteen years prior, my dear friend Dr. Ongley said to me, "If you remember nothing else in life remember this: Only thinking makes it so." Many have spoken about the power of thought and its expansion in the Universe like a boomerang—it must come back to us for all to stay in balance and harmony. This is the law of physics on this planet Earth.

Vibrating at twelve has to do with pulling away from others and fully trusting in the self. Thoughts become even more powerful, sending Energy out of the field and the field responding in kind. This is the universal law. The problem usually is that when it comes back we are the victim —"Someone did it to me."

At fourteen, the ten and twelve blend together but at even higher power levels. During this phase I needed more time to be alone, getting to know myself in a new way. Fourteen is also the higher self or soul connection. It is very centering and creates a profound sense of wholeness. Learning to see through the eyes of the soul takes commitment and much practice. It is like learning a new language in silence with no one to practice with.

The vibration of fifteen, sixteen, seventeen, and eighteen are not for the light-hearted; they are about the ego. The first phase is busting the ego, a process that takes outrageous acts of humility and a feeling of total powerlessness. I was stuck here for many months. Then there is the bringing in of a new and healthy ego. Much turmoil came with this and the people in my immediate environment suffered. Some did not know what to do and were very worried. Paul, my then-husband, used to say the mother ship would be there to pick me up anytime now. Little did he know how accurate this statement was.

The vibration of nineteen is the beginning of our connection with other life forms, and twenty connects us forever with all dimensions and gives us free ET wi-fi with all its information. This was a fun, wild, E-ticket ride and sometimes a bit on the spooky side that was hard on the mind. I saw miracles everywhere. At times the heavens would light up, sending a message I could hear in my mind. It was always in a loud male or female voice in my mind being very insistent, repeating the same message over and over until I did as I was told. I experienced several ships in the sky and witnessed the effect they had on anything electrical. For several months a voice, the same voice, spoke to me loudly every night between 2:00 and 3:00 AM and tell me to go outside, or sit in a certain chair, or get some water to drink. All sorts of different things. Many things I can't remember and time simply disappeared. It was a disorienting time but it was part of the process and I knew on a subtle level much rewiring and downloading of information took place for me. There was an adjustment in the crystalline structure of my brain and also a rearranging of DNA bringing new codes forward.

I was remembering more and more and felt peaceful. I feel humbled and blessed in this life to have access to Divine avatars and dear friends in vibrationally higher places who protect me during my own personal hurricane. I saw and communicated with all three of my oldest grandsons before they were born and participated in the birthing experience, merging with their souls and welcoming them. The grandest of all experiences. All newborns should be helped and hear a whisper of a voice welcoming them by saying, "You are so loved."

In my dreams I was shown scientific symbols, codes, sounds, and a blending of colors and how to use them. My computer is filled with information that, like a puzzle, has many missing pieces. My dreams were about Mother Meera and Paramatman but I could not see his Light. Mother Meera said, "Paramatman is the supreme Light. It is inside of everything and outside of everything. Life is unmanifested and love is manifested. God is Generator, Operator, and Destroyer. God is Energy that moves and creates, sustains, and recreates out of itself."

. . .

God is too big to understand in the mind, I've come to learn. God, you can only *feel* to know. God is feeling. Some think that he is some big genius who figures everything out. (Here, as I typed this, I heard loud laughter.) God is smart because he feels. Everything in the Universe feels but it does not all think. Be in nature, be in the clouds, fly with the birds, hear the wind if you want to feel God. *Feel me and you will remember where home is.* Over time, religions have made up their own stories about "God" and have personalized him as their God and how theirs is the best and others have the wrong God. It is all quite hysterical. The ego of man. It serves its purpose and wars are still fought using God as the excuse for greed and wealth by the few ruling this planet.

If God were speaking to you he would say, *"When you pray you talk to me and when you meditate I talk to you."*

As time passed, the daily routine of life became more of a challenge because it was new and unfamiliar until I began to learn to find joy in the silliest things. The vibration of twenty to twenty-one are all chakra work—learning to pump energy out in a constant flow instead of depending on others to fill you. Like the story of the cup and saucer. Always have a full cup, letting the overflow in the saucer be what you share with others in need.

. . .

The vibration of the thirties is about becoming your own Energy source. These were wonderful times. I learned to create, open, and close Energy vortexes, and my healing work became magical and easy. I learned to see with other eyes and I noticed that manifesting was easy and very fast. I had to be careful here because we will get what we focus on and then we must bear it.

The vibrations of the forties and the fifties are about instant manifestation and magic, the kids of experiences and gifts for which we do not yet have language in this dimension. This can be a very lonely time, but on the other hand, how can we be lonely when we are a part of everything everywhere?

Knowing the human has the potential to achieve a level of sixty-four vibrations feels like a mountain so steep with the peak too high to see and I was but a mere speck. Looking at my grandson Tyler, who was eight months old and desperate to see and get to everything, I could only chuckle at myself and my thoughts of impatience as I saw this reflected in his eyes. Once on the path, the magic of it makes time truly vanish.

I am thankful for everything and have learned to feel the subtle vibrations in all things. Chaos slides past me and what-ever comes my way from the everyday world has nothing to stick to. It is all a reflection and another way for me to learn and grow.

ETHEREUM GOLD

Ethereum gold has had a very powerful effect on me. For me, it feels like there is a powerful electrical charge behind my thoughts. I feel that I am in control of my intentions in a more powerful way. Manifestation, at times, occur in an instant.

Ethereum gold is a sacred powder, a unique natural trace mineral deposit with electromagnetic frequencies and wave patterns that raise the vibration of the natural Energy fields in the body. As the human frequency in our body-spirit increases, the vibrational difference between our thoughts and the object of our thoughts is reduced. Therefore, the time required to manifest on the physical plane is often cur down. The gold decreases the space-time continuum. It also breaks down restrictive and repetitive patterns at the cellular level and opens up possibilities not previously considered.

The gold is a link between science and spirituality. There are magical properties in the monatomic elements of the powder. They are single element structures in a very high spin state with properties to assist in transformation as a super conductor on a cellular level. When the electromagnetic frequency lab tested the soil, the lab reported two wave patterns, clockwise and counter-clockwise, going to the center and blending into one as in the Divine force. Tested through laser photogenic neutron activation methods (a 300-second burn test) to get the monotonic elements in the gold, Dr. Kelly, a scientist specializing in electromagnetic frequencies for over twenty-five years, said about Ethereum gold: "This material seems to divide its Energy into two oppositely projected units, then the wave forms carry a close resemblance to the body's Energy channels referred to as: white spirals: pinball Nadi, solar dark spirals: ida Nadi lunar."

There seems to be high electrical potential created around the sample, with high-standing waves being produced. Information that makes up the human body unit could be translated (moved) in time and space when this material is ingested.

An implosion of Earth pushed this material to the surface of the earth for us at the time. Egyptian books of the dead speak of a white gold that transformed and assisted in the transition of the body at death into the other world. I have heard references to Ethereum gold containing the possibility to activate human consciousness.

Upon opening the king's chamber, a white powder was found in the coffer containing rhodium and iridium, two elements secreted by the pituitary and pineal glands from the Theta brain wave states in meditation. The culmination of the Egyptian initiations was transformation into the Christ consciousness and a stable light body, able to walk between two worlds. Perhaps the gold powder is a gentle help in that direction, appropriate for these times where our life is the initiation and our body is the sacred temple. Raising the intention and the electromagnetic vibration can possibly create the paradigm shift that allows the human to focus on health, being disease-free, and taking responsibility for its creation. The secret codes containing all information can be found in different vibrations of sound, color, geometric shapes, numbers, and even mathematical equations. As we all become more conscious, more will be revealed to activate our own innate cellular memory.

Ours is a very exciting time with the potential for tremendous progress as a species. It would be much easier if so much information was not hidden from us or inaccurately conveyed to those who run with everything they hear. We must each take responsibility to research and find the mysteries for optimal life. It is all at our disposal if we look deep below the surface.

---

1. Atwater, P.M.H. *Future memory*, 2013. Hampton Roads Publishing.

Chapter Five

ENERGETIC VIBRATIONS AND HEALING

The Universe and the Body Electrical

Seventy years ago science discovered the Universe was electrical in nature. Molecules are held together by electrical charges. Atoms are dynamic electrical packages occupying space. Neutrons, protons, and electrons are all electrically charged. The further you go into your own micro universe, the more you realize your body is just layer upon layer of electrical construct. You just appear to be solid in matter! Actually, your body is a Milky Way of tiny interwoven electrical patterns. It's one hundred percent electrical construct. This must be understood if we are to become healthy and hold the capacity to double our life span.

In spite of it all, we still identify with our labels. I am Jane, a schoolteacher, a mother, I drive a BMW and live in Redondo Beach and I am a Muslim. Surprise—that last label didn't fit in your mind, right? What does it all mean? This is all an illusion. The labels come from our parents and whoever our influences were before the age of seven (this is when the hard drive of our biological computer our flesh and bones is imprinted and off we go). This is now me and I and my ego is in the driver's seat.

We are only conscious states of awareness and we experience our so-called reality through our band of frequency through this biological computer. We are completely controlled by our identifying with our labels.

When Jane dies, is she still a Muslim or a schoolteacher?

Once the hard drive is in place the I that we identify with becomes our "normal." This is handed to us from birth and we had no input whatsoever. Perception comes from information received and this again comes from what is in the hard drive. Fault lines of hate and abuse that were created for us now *control* us. Our belief systems about everything are cemented in place. Now come our assumptions about ourselves, other people, the world, and our place in it. From here we have thoughts and behavior, which then create the results that show up in our everyday experience. Where is the magic, where is the ability to manifest anything through our intentions? Our filters are clogged with conditioned information and repetitive behavior. We cannot see through clear, fresh, innocent eyes but only through the many layers of experience. This creates the same things in our life over and over again. Nothing changes. We grow old, sick, depressed, die, and are forgotten.

Humans have several things in common. We believe that material accumulation is all that matters and that life has to be a struggle if we are ever going to achieve anything. Our brain is said to be like an iPod and can only create from the hard drive. A Newtonian belief says invisible fields shape matter. If this is so, our minds may be able to override the hard drive and shape the world so we can change.

People get stuck and create much misery for ourselves. For example, cancer is in my family so I must also have the gene for it and will surely get it. This of course is ridiculous when you simply change your mind about this assumption. Humans rape the planet in an attempt to gather more than the next guy as a measure of success. The problem is it is never enough and never stops. Our world is always in crisis, in fear. We shut down and accept this. We are made of fifty trillion cells and like fifty trillion people, each has a job to do. We put much

Energy into not allowing them to do their work. We live in a world of the fittest wins, competition, wars, famines, child trafficking, selling of organs, massive drug consumption, and Big Pharma with no cures, only massive profits. We are slowly dying in these illusionary constraints of competition. And our world would thrive in an instant if this was flipped over into *co-operation*.

But this is our reality, all because our mind is controlled and our hard drive cemented in at such an early age—and so completely—that we don't even know we're in our own way and that everything that we think we are came from other people.

It is possible to live an extraordinary life. This is hard work and requires a great commitment. It is time to know that living an extraordinary life is possible and fulfillment is a personal art form. When passion reigns in life, time flies; there's no time for drama, sickness, victimhood, and there is no time to care what others think of you. Body, mind, and spirit is in perfect alignment and balance.

In this state of passion, you feel stoned yet never use the substance. Being judged has no impact because you are always stoned with life. Go inside yourself. The body is the greatest chemical factory. You are but the manager. You are not a consequence of the good opinions of others.

Humanity, however, keeps digging deeper instead of beginning to understand we are all and there is nothing to find. Our toolbox is full but we look for the key—yet the box is not even locked.

The ancient Greeks thought our Universe was made of tiny blocks that produced all substances. That idea still haunts many today. Scientists keep digging into the substance of the Universe, seeking that elusive basic particle of matter and, just when we think we have it, we realize it's not a particle at all. Instead it's a moving structure of electrical charges. The sun is ninety-three million miles from the earth. But make an atom to scale of the solar system and the electrons are forty-seven times farther from the nucleus than the earth is from the sun. Instead of a building block, the atom is ninety-nine percent empty space.

If this is not a mind blower let us add to this that humans think they are the greatest life form in the Universe. There are life forms in the trillions of galaxies and may all be held up to some extent by the malfunction and limitations of humanity on Earth.

. . .

Let's move forward with the complexities of things that we so love. Atoms are minute electric patterns or matrices occupying space. Scientists now know the atom's pieces aren't *pieces*—a proton is not solid and the neutron is actually electrical inside, neutral only on the surface. The most grand example of electricity is watching a lightning storm. The richness and intensity of that Light may be the closest we come to our God source, yet many fear it. Might this not be the power inside each of us?

Toxins are also emotions of anger, rage, fear, worry, grief, hatred of self, which are trapped in the organs of the body that hold the specific emotion. As mentioned earlier, fear lives in the kidneys and bladder, anger in liver and gall bladder, grief is held in the large intestine, and worry in the pancreas, spleen, and stomach. A book teaching us the language of our body and how it speaks to us through the emotions in our systems would be the solution to more than we know right now.

You can clearly see that we need a new understanding and learn to release and clean house. The human needs the nutrients in a package the body can accept. You can look to enzymes, psychology, biochemistry, herbs...that's fine. But if they are not originated to the electrical universe that drives and controls our body's process, they will unravel in chaos and continue the health failures of our last century. Most things are artificially produced, preserved, and contaminated, adding only toxins to the mind-body connection. We have been ingesting vitamins and nutrients that our internal electrical universe did not recognize, causing premature aging, disease, and premature death. The vast knowledge and scientific data available to us now reveals our true electrical and unseen nature, and we must change our thinking and start treating the body as the electrical construct that it is.

ENERGETIC VIBRATIONS, THE KEY TO HEALING

It has been said that disease is a battle of vibrations. Energy in its many forms and many frequencies of vibration is at the root of all things. It transcends time and space and can never be destroyed. Some of this Energy vibrates at a very low level and can be seen by the humans as matter. It is only a slow-moving atom.

Were we to speed up the vibration of matter beyond the human's ability to see, then we see only what appears to be space. If we could move the atoms in the table to a high-spinning frequency, the table would—*poof!*—disappear before our eyes. It's easy to see the extent and the ease with which we can be mind controlled and made to feel in most aspects of our dense reality. Already we are driven by the fear created all around us. Remember there is only love. When we are neutral and untouched by outside-driven fear-based emotions, work environments, religion, toxic people, events, brutal deaths, wars, and the daily news, then we can be free.

By some, all this is called magic. Is it really? The scientist has now concluded that he has broken the atom down as far as is possible and all there is, is Energy. Actually this is all there ever was and we came full circle to reach this profound conclusion.

The great Nikola Tesla said, "The day science begins to study non-physical phenomena, it will make more progress in one decade than in all the previous centuries of its existence." Many scientists and doctors today are ostracized for speaking their truth. A true scientist agrees to spend time uncovering the truth even if he does not understand how it fits in with what he has been taught. Unfortunately many do not want to know; they are comfortable in their little world and want nothing to upset their ivory tower.

Dr. Bevan Reid, a lecturer in obstetrics and gynecology at the University of Sydney, believes that he has the evidence from repeated experiments to prove there is an electromagnetic force around all living matter, and that this force can induce changes in cells without chemical interaction. The reaction to this theory was total disbelief and he is ignored by his peers. What he is really saying is that we can work through the electromagnetic field to heal people instead of pumping them full of chemicals. Tesla would be applauding him from on high, saying, Now they can begin the new decade when they will make some real progress. Whoever said that minds are like parachutes—they can only function when they are open—certainly knew what he was talking about.

This field Energy has been photographed for a long time but the mere idea that this field can affect changes in cells without medically prescribed drugs is the last straw. Let's look at the reason for this. This simple and inexpensive way of leading as awake and functioning life would bring chaos to many areas of our establishments. It means that our present bandage mentality of healing through drugs, medicines, chemicals radiating the body (sometimes to death), directly injecting chemicals into the blood, sucking the marrow out of the bones, or filling the body with metal hardware that will surely and permanently cut the energetic flow that is vital to life, is supposed to restore the body to health.

As long as this is the only form of treatment worthy of attention, in the name of saving the human condition, the multibillion-dollar drug companies throughout the world will continue to be exactly that: multibillion-dollar drug companies. Can you imagine if science followed Dr. Reid in his findings—that it was no longer necessary to pollute the body with nasty chemicals, and that much better results were supported by working through the electromagnetic force surrounding all life matter—what would happen?

Who do you suppose provides the funding that keeps thousands upon thousands of these scientists in their cushy little jobs in their laboratories searching for new and better drugs? You guessed it—the same multibillion dollar drug companies. Science has been conditioned to focus on drugs, not wellness. This is the vicious cycle and the human pays the price. We buy the drugs and a large portion of our taxes are passed on to these companies as well. Approximately one third of our elderly patients—a huge population today—are in hospitals being treated for problems caused by previous medicines given to them by the doctor, to whom we give our power.

As previously mentioned, disease is a battle of vibrations. When a group of cells are out of balance, they are vibrating at the wrong frequency and are in need of Energy in order to bring them to their correct frequency. There are many ways to do this.

There is a healing with color. If white light is split, we see different colors. Are we not simply seeing different vibrations of Light? The Energy centers or chakras in our body are different colors and do respond to like vibrations for balance. Likewise, in sound therapy, sound waves of a specific wavelength are used to alter the individual's cell vibratory patterns and restore them to health. Homeopathy, originally discovered by Samuel Hahnemann early in the last century, works in the principle of like treating like. Again, it is at its core of a balancing vibration to restore balance in the body. It has been proven that a photograph reprinted over hundreds of times still carries with it the same vibration that it had from the person when it was taken. This is how many can hold someone's photograph and tell you all about the person. It is simply an ability to pick up and read the vibration.

Increasing the human vibration is vital for us all at this time because we will lift ourselves above our limitations and can now perform what some call miracles. For many, miracles appear outside of universal law. There is merely a higher level of law that may be activated by those who earned the qualifications to use them.

It is our time now to become more Divine. Our bodies are not meant to be born, diseased, and die—we are multidimensional in nature, and hopefully the honored place for medicine in the future is one of focusing on health and balance by working with energetic vibration. Governments have been using this for eons. As we reach out with love to all mankind, love will flow like water in a stream, and its high vibration will alter the cells that are out of balance and give way to health and harmony throughout the body.

. . .

Unfortunately, there are many on the earth who have no idea about vibrational frequencies and Energy-raising yet. Life is about the daily routine of groceries, laundry, climbing the ladder of success, getting good grades from a dysfunctional system, vacation, weekends, and the drama of family and the community. Like a horse with blinders on in a race, the human window of dimensional experience is deadened by the belief there is no more. This is as good as it gets for me. Until they choose to explore and discover who they truly are, they will continue on their incarnation path until they do. Eventually all must go there to discover the great potential within, which has been dormant for long. Why not go there now? It is the greatest ride our Universe has ever seen.

OUR COLLECTIVE INITIATION

Over two thousand years ago, the ancients spoke of changes within and around the earth. In the last few years the vibration of the earth has increased in unbelievable proportions. The magnetic frequencies coming from its core affect us all in ways that are unfamiliar. Our relationships are changing or falling apart, sleep patterns are altered, cellular and DNA structures are changing. For some, chakras are blending from seven into two, and our perception of time has put many in a state of chaos, confusion, and stress. Systems are not working and are in a state of entropy. The cosmic waves hitting the planet are also new and have a high spin vibration. Shows like

Grimm are preparing us to get familiar with shape shifting. Many on the planet are challenged in holding their human form. Many feel squeezed between a rock and a hard place.

The human experience has always been directly related to density in and around the earth. We are surrounded by ancient technology and special chambers, and underground cities all over the globe. The obvious examples may be the Great Pyramid of Giza, where the upper chambers hold lower magnetic vibrations. This environment is a null-magnetic field. In it, we have direct access to pure information because we are able to drop patterns of judgement, fear, ego, and the lag of time between thoughts. This experience can also be created by us, increasing our own vibration. The door is now open on our planet and it is time to take a giant step and create an attitude of excitement as we choose, with our free will, to accept cellular and core level changes.

As each initiate chooses to think and feel differently, allowing the fullest expression of being, available only in the moment, you become the living model of what was taught in the initiation chambers for the last 11,000 years. Your life is in preparation for the great Shift. You are living the initiation as you read these pages and must release, grow, and embrace with joy every change and experience. This path will lead us all to the One, whatever God you believe in. In our initiation we sometimes mess up the lessons of our life experience and die in learning. Others who do learn and survive the final test as this conscious cycle comes to completion experience each cell in the physical body vibrating with a higher and higher frequency. When moving into our etheric double, or light body, ascension is complete. Our purpose is to pierce the veil of life's mystery. Our cells beat with the pulsed heartbeat of Earth and we must reconnect with her vibration.

The ancients created electrical balance, through crystalline healing, which is equal to our connection with Mother Earth. As the vibration bottoms out, the great event predicted by religious tradition, Nostradamus, Edgar Cayse, and other seers for thousands of years will be ours to experience. The chaos leading up to this time will cease. The poles of the earth will reverse and we must be prepared to match the new and much higher vibration. This is now the New Age and full of realization of our multidimensionality in other dimension. It is, however, important to go to our *inner*net for answers and stop exposing ourselves to news, politics, and all who create fear in our time here on Earth.

MERKABA, THE VEHICLE OF OUR LIGHT BODY

References to *Merkaba* have been limited to the mystery schools, shamanistic initiations, and some religious doctrines. The Merkaba is an energetic field that surrounds each cell, the body, and is also outside of the body. The name is found both in Egyptian and Hebrew languages. *Mer* is light; *ka* is spirit; *ba* is body. It can be thought of as a vehicle, not limited by time, space, or dimensions. This is not, however, separate from us and has a specific key resonance aligned with our cellular structure and light body.

In *The Keys of Enoch*, by J.J. Hurtak, it is said that Merkabah appears in many forms; it can be seen as a pure energy envelope of light, it can take on any membrane or color appearance to correspond with you and guide you into other experiences of creation. Through this connection, various lights are linked together, allowing vehicles to travel between various dimensions and galaxies. We are on the path of being in light body and being in the Merkaba vehicle.

Imagine the Merkaba as an airplane. You are on a huge bus filled with people driving toward the plane. You get out and enter the plane. Where will you sit? You can choose any seat you want. Take a moment and see yourself in the position of your choice. The chosen spot for you gives you a hint as to where you are consciously as you read this. Are you in the first seat, the middle, the back, an aisle seat, window? Are you a stewardess, the pilot? The vehicle speaks to us through light consciousness forms, by energizing the cosmic pulsations to pierce the earth's electromagnetic fields.

Merkaba can project itself from one life system or galaxy to the life system or galaxy of other universes. The power of the Merkaba proceeds directly from the mind, which has merged with the One. *Enoch* explained that just as the mind through faith healing can directly concentrate its brain waves on a finger or a foot cell; it can also project healing through a light circulatory grid built into the heart. The One uses laser-like radiations to project Energy from the Merkaba vehicle and our light body, into our system for the education of the human self and/or the repairing of our programs. The Merkaba also brings prophetic consciousness from one level to the other levels of creation. Without this, the human could not merge into the One.

When man has evolved into a greater understanding of Light, he will use equations of spiritual Energy which will give him the ability to travel through space. Other universes will give him the teachings and education of the One regarding higher evolution, which is to be shared with the community on Earth. The Merkaba cannot be seen it comes from higher coding of Light, and steps down in vibration to enter our third dimension. The Energy field of the vehicle can appear as a pulsating pyramid, a pentagon, or a Star of David.

By going through multiple lights and complicated triangular coordinates, it keys into certain time periods of the species growth and development. In our time of consciousness, Merkaba will cast its twelve spiral radiations of pyramidal right Energy upon us and we will lift up into great joy and liberation.

In Gregg Braden's *Awakening to Zero Point* he mentions that a powerful symbol deep within the spiral of rotation is deeply engrained within the conscious matrix of mankind.

"It is in the field of the Merkaba that is described and coded in the most famous work of Leonardo da Vinci's drawings; from his mystery school; that of proportions of the human figure. The focus of the drawing is the frontal form of a man with his legs and arms spread to positions at key angles and enclosed within a circle superimposed upon a square. The angle of the arms is that of the ratio of five divided by two. This is the identical angle of the diagonal from corner to corner within the king's chamber of the Great Pyramid—an initiation site of Merkaba technology."

As we move through our life experience, complete balance within and without must be achieved so that we may walk with one foot in the physical and one foot in spirit. As our consciousness becomes aware of Merkaba, it will assist us in remembering that balance is vital and it helps us in control-ling our response to our external world. We simply learn to vibrate, mind, body, and soul into the higher source of information, changing our response to viruses, bacteria, toxins, radiation and the future shift of the earth.

Please don't confuse this with the government's made up story about global warming. It is simply a cover for their inability to control the weather.

Chapter Six

THE BODY, MIND, AND SOUL CONNECTION

If peace on this Earth is what we are striving for, then we must each look at what we have created so far and how.

Over time, the vibrations coming from the humans in this third dimension been primarily negative in nature. They have come from fear, judgement, anger, war, killing, ego, power, and a need for human control with and a me-me attitude. Included in this negativity going into the Universe we must include atomic testing and other pollutants.

When these vibrations move into the cosmic dimensions, the balance between our world and the cosmic world become out of balance. The scale in the Universe that holds the third dimension on one side and the cosmic sea on the other becomes heavy with negativity; in order to be in balance with itself, the cosmic sea releases the destructive negative vibrations and feeds them back to our world causing more negativity, wars, diseases, and chaos.

It is time for us to grow up and realize that we are one with the God force, and that what we do and think is all a mirror of ourselves. We have freedom of choice but not freedom of consequence. The earth herself has suffered and is mourning her abuse. She is shedding this pain by violent weather changes, volcanoes, Earth changes, and the eventual axis shift. Since we as humans are one with the earth we too feel this internal writhing and the need to shed and to cleansing.

In order to have balance between the two universes, we must be in harmony with all things and in balance internally so that the vibrations we send out are positive and carry the vibration of love, which is the One. Then we can bathe in the return of this vibration in kind. It should be our *goal* to raise the human vibration in kind. It should be our goal to raise the human vibration and to move closer and closer to our light body, which is within and also in the other dimension. It is where we hang out half of our life while asleep yet we are totally unaware. This is our link.

. . .

There is much work to do. Let us look at ways and techniques that would assist us in this ascension.

RELEASING LOWER VIBRATIONS

First, we must become fully aware of each atom, each molecule, each cell, each group of cells, each organ, each group of organs, which are our body's systems. When we are aware of all vibrations of our being then we can begin the creation in our third dimension.

Second, we begin the process by creative thinking and picturing clearly what we want to create in this dimension. The intention must be clear and strong. Create this and hold the picture in the third eye. The picture of the intention must be clear, in full color, and in the vibration of who you are.

Third, move this picture into the base or root chakra, hold it there, and experience the essence of who you are. In the root chakra of your body you will feel its vibration. Know yourself as it and it as you.

The fourth step is to bring the vibrational picture into the entire body and feel the vibration within. There is no difference between the physical vibration of the picture and you.

. . .

Lastly move the picture into the One and release it. This is where the essence of creation is. The Universe aligns with your creation and it shows up in the world.

You have now manifested your thought. This can be taught and used as a tool.

CLEARING EMOTIONS IN THE PHYSICAL BODY

There are many modalities that clear and balance, if the person chooses. Reflexology is a great way to discover where emotions are trapped and what those emotions are. Each organ vibrates to a different frequency and color. The feet contain acupressure points that will tell the story; this is very helpful. Clearing meridian flow allows the Energy to move freely, as well as Acupuncture and the many other physical disciplines.

The Indigo biofeedback system in person or remotely is probably the most concise and all-encompassing of them all. Massage, cranial balancing, Rolfing, and lymph drainage are other examples which may facilitate the release.

The brain can be stimulated through the eyes by color and the ears with sound, the nose with aromatherapy. Because the physical sensors are directly related to the

brain this is the easiest way to change the energetic vibratory field.

Another very important aspect of moving into light body is
the development of the thymus, the seat of the rejuvenation
process and it must grow. You may want to do a thymus
thump by tapping it three times each day. It is located in the
center of the chest, approximately where the breastbone
ends, an inch or so under the heart but in the center.

THE IMPORTANCE OF CLEARING THE BODY'S ELECTROMAGNETIC FIELD

I want to put this very simply because it is a critically important message and I hope will stimulate you into thought and
action. In a personal initiation with a Divine mother, an
avatar, I sat at her feet in a beautiful garden filled with wild-
flowers in Santa Fe, New Mexico. Speaking softly and lovingly,
she shared many secrets about life, the Universe, the sound of
the wind, the sound of the flowers, sacred geometric symbols,
and an hour filled with bliss so words cannot do justice to the
moment. This is what I remember that had a profound
impact on me and will one day be the key to health for us all.

Patterns of disease appear in the electromagnetic field around
the body as long as six months before they manifest in the
physical form. I will leave you with the ramifications of that
statement. Stop and give this much thought.

IN THE BEGINNING GOD CREATED TWELVE VIBRATIONS

As new scientific information comes forth, mankind will see that the door to total health and moving fully into Divinity may be unlocked once we understand these twelve vibrations. The individual frequencies carry a code in the form of a specific symbol, a specific color, and a specific sound. Once these are unlocked, healing takes place when the individual's vibration is paired with one of the twelve vibrations, which is in the same frequencies.

By using the combination of sound, color, and symbol we can easily keep the electromagnetic field and the six-foot physical field around our body clear so that God's Light is the only thing that occupies the human space. The Light is pure information and we will finally remember and be one with the Divine.

I have been shown some of these symbols and given some information. This can only mean that I was tapping into the mass consciousness, a field of infinite possibilities. The universal truth has only one desire: to be born.

Since 1928, medicine has experienced many milestones. This began with British bacteriologist Alexander Fleming who was discarding cultures which were left on his workbench while vacationing. A mold-like fungus had grown in mass and when he studied the plate he noticed that the mold had destroyed an entire range of producing bacteria. Penicillin, the first antibiotic, was discovered.

In 1953 the double helix in DNA was discovered be geneticist James Watson and Francis Crick. In 1955 Albert Sabin and James Salk created a polio vaccine. In the 1960s Dr. Christiaan Barnard performed the first human heart transplant and the '70s gave us the CAT scan, the first test tube baby, and the eradication of smallpox. The 1980s uncovered the aids virus and the '90s are called a dazzling time since they include the art of arthroscopic surgery, effective chemotherapy, and highly specialized drug treatments. All this is wonderful and plays an important part in the transformation of the human species. Along with these discoveries have come bigger and better drugs for all scenarios. When I hear the term *effective chemotherapy* I can only wonder what that means. Yes, a mass of cells have died but so has the patient. It is critical that we wake up to the horrors going on right in front of our eyes.

Chapter Seven

CONCLUSION

Our human experience began in a Divine environment of Earth and sun. Changes in weather corresponds with seasons and natural cycles. They impact our human rhythm and keep us in tune with Mother Nature and the pulsation of the cosmic sea.

Our physicality was stimulated by the natural electromagnetic fields in our environment, namely nature, Earth, planets, lightning, and ionic discharges. Life was simple, filled with ritual and worship of the Divine.

The human has created for himself, in the name of progress, an environment that artificially impinges on his Divine connection. The man-made electromagnetic energies are silent and invisible but are vibrations pulsing in all our modern conveniences. As we scan our homes and workplaces we find low-voltage offenders which are detrimental to our electromagnetic field and our health: vacuum cleaners, stereos, air conditioning, electric clocks, heating pads, electric blankets, television, radio, fluorescent lighting, hair dryers, shavers, curling irons, telephones, answering machines, fax machines, computers, iPads, microwaves, refrigerators, and anything else that is plugged into our AC current.

The low 60Hz vibration creates stress, suppresses the immune system, affects the heart and our mental cognition. Add to this the constant fear generated in world events and political distress; this pretty much covers our physical bases. It is interesting to note all the immune deficiency diseases on our planet now. Epstein-Barr is one that is widespread and seldom apparent or diagnosed. Add to all this our modern diet of convenience. Food is nuked to perfection filled with fat, sugar, artificial preservatives, and additives. This has led us to a dull and drone-like society. As a species we have become depressed, powerless, lethargic, victimized, stressed, and frustrated, and the dysfunctional wheel is placed on a talk show and the news media.

Free will has escaped us; we have lost touch with nature and worship artificial gods. Our focus is on gathering props that make us look good on the surface. By changing our zip code and creating high drama in our life we distract ourselves and feel stimulated in that moment.

We can get back to basics by willingly choosing consciousness. We can learn to understand and feel that we are Energy which is in a constant state of vibration. We can tune into the natural rhythm of our environment and surround ourselves with higher electromagnetic frequencies that counterbalance the detrimental man-made vibrations. Once in balance vibrationally, our choices for health, diet, relationships, career, and place of residence will come from our soul's choice and Divine knowing.

No one can change us but us. It is our responsibility and it is time now to make a choice. The choice is to be awake in our human experience or asleep. Each one must connect with the Divine Source, that from which we came.

"I am a little pencil in God's hands. He does the thinking. He does the writing."
Mother Theresa

We are kept in the dark about what is really going on in all aspects of life. Wake up. With the internet, you can research everything: the human cloning with other species, the mind control, trafficking of children and adults for sex and many other horrors that are kept from us. We are intentionally distracted by the ridiculous news and chatter about nonsense when the real story lies deep below the shallow pool we are allowed to live in. I say jump in and dive deep.

I know this might be difficult for some to hear but we choose our disease. Science will understand the importance of discovering why a patient chooses something and how it can be diagnosed in its early stages in the electromagnetic field and how like frequencies heal like frequency diseases. This theory has worked for many years in homeopathy. All pain or disease serves the patient; it reinforces emotional belief systems of love, self-worth, victimization, and a disconnection from the Divine Source. This is when we are no more than a flock of sheep controlled by one man with a stick and one dog.

If these belief systems could be reinforced in other ways and with early diagnosis of emotional well-being, there would be no need to be sick. There would be no point. The biggest problem facing us all is that there is too much money in drugs, an industry that has its long tentacles deeply entrenched in science, government, the medical community and our very homes. Is it any wonder that when a hospice patient is signed on for care, all medications are stopped and in most cases after two weeks the patient gets better. But by then it is too late or it is just the patient's time to move on and live in a different set of clothing.

It is time to look from behind the veil of illusion of illusion that has kept us informed and manipulated. The cure for disease is not in the drug. The answer is in the body, mind, and soul connection. Today we have a doctor, medicine, and body connection.

Turn to the Divine and be guided and health and joy will be seen in your eyes. The change will be made as the masses turn toward personal transformation and power . They will not put up with it anymore. More and more people are turning toward alternative solutions for health and balance in all areas of life.

Health is but a vibration away.

Chapter Eight

FURTHER READING

FURTHER READING

Becker, Robert, MD and Selton, Gary, *The Body Electric*, 1985. New York, NY: Quill.

Becker, Robert, MD, *Cross Currents*, 1990. New York, NY: Putman Books.

Braden, Gregg, *Awaken to Zero Point*, 1993. Question, NM: Braun-Brumfield Inc.

Chopra, Deepak, MD, *Creating Health*, 1987. Boston, MA: Houghton Mifflin Company.

Dossey, Larry, MD, *Prayer is Good Medicine*. San Francisco, CA: Harper Collins.

Dumitrescu, Ion, MD and Kenyon, Julian, MD, *Electro-*

magnetic Imaging in Medicine & Biology, 1979. Bucharest: Scientific & Encyclopedic Publishing House.

Gerber, Richard, MD, *Vibrational Medicine*, 1988. Santa Fe, NM: Bear & Company.

Hurtak, J.J., *The Keys of Enoch*, 1977. Los Gatos, CA: The Academy of Future Sciences.

Kalwit, Holer, *Dreamtime and Inner Space*, 1988. Boston, MA: Shambala Publications.

Lambert, Collin, *You Too Can Heal*, 1993. Tauranga, New Zealand: Peaceful Living Publications.

Liberman, Jacob, *Light, Medicine of the Future*, 1991. Santa Fe, NM: Bear & Company.

Manning, Clark A., MD and Vanrenen, Louis J., MD, *Bioenergetic Medicines East and West*, 1988. Berkeley, CCA: North Atlantic Books.

Russel, Walter, *The Secret of Light*, 1947. Swannanoa, Waynesboro, VA: University of Science & Philosophy.

Solara, *How to Live on a Small Planet*, 1996 Whitefish, MT: Star: Borne Unlimited.

Tachi-ren, Tashira, *What is Light Body?* 1996. Livermore, CA: Oughten House Publications.

Icke, David, *Phantom Self*, 2016. Isle of Wight British Library.

Adilakshmi, *The Mother*. Thalheim, Germany: Mother Meera Publications.

Hawkins, R. David, MD, PhD, *The Eye of the I*, 2001. Sedona, AZ: Veritas Publishing Company.

Yogananda, Paramahansa, *Man's Eternal Quest*, 1955. Los

Angeles, CA: Self-Realization Fellowship, International Publishing Council.

Made in the USA
Monee, IL
13 October 2021

79964786R20060